HAZE OF LATTER DAYS

Theory and Picturestrip by
Karen Kellock Ph.D.

This is a new theory in psychology. According to Koestler, all landmark theories are presented in picture-strip format (right-left integration) to bring on the "aha" experience of the formula (the characteristic of all new paradigms).

FORMULA FOR THEORY:

ALL SUCCESS ATTRACTION
ALL DISEASE OBSTRUCTION
ALL RECOVERY ELIMINATION

The three obstructions are:
people, habit and food.

Remove your obstruction and
you snap to your goals,
waiting in the wings.

HAZE OF THE LATTER DAYS

If liberals are the heart of the democratic party it's really dirty. And if you express a conservative opinion you'll be put on a black list and made an unemployable minion. We must now parrot that progressive consensus or lose everything (it's expensive). Modern worldview: "I can't abide any thought other than my own". No wonder they accept weirdness, badness--look at Harry Potter queerness/madness: a sign of the latter days as societies go down in a haze. Just stay away: They're so gross and unrefined you could never explain so just escape.

NEVER AGAIN

THE UNGRATEFUL
USING YOU FOR PERSONAL GAIN
THE SILENT TREATMENT [STONEWALLING]
BE ON THE WATCH ALWAYS
NARC TACTICS/YOUR REACTIONS
WALK AWAY, NEVER ENDURE
WHY ARE YOU KEEPING THEM?
LOVEBOMBING OF PSYCHOPATHS
KEEP EM OUT ONCE GONE
WONDERFUL RELIEF OF LETTING GO

NEVER AGAIN

THE UNGRATEFUL

The catalyst for great wealth is gratitude for what you have but the narc only focuses on his lack.

No matter what you've given him the narcissist focuses on what you haven't: what a conundrum.

The covert narcissist has learned over time what to mimic like "I'm grateful" but it's a gimmick.

Never trust someone due to a sweet smile or all the right words cuz narcs are experts at that first.

Since the narc only focuses on what he lacks, he feels only jealousy when you get ahead: fact.

Covert narcs won't admit mistakes cuz they don't like confrontation being PASSIVE [-aggressive].

USING YOU FOR PERSONAL GAIN

They are masters at using you for personal gain [the greatest manipulators at getting you to pay].

Whether it's climbing the corporate ladder or getting you to pay for dinner, they're masterful winners.

They WORM their way into homes to gain control [2 Tim 3:6]. Put boundaries on em and you're a foe.

Narcs are easily agitated. Something you said or implied even if innocent they see as snide.

The slightest criticism or things no going their way seems to incite an out of control child ok.

NEVER AGAIN

Narcs have low coping skills. It doesn't take much to set em off then play victim [head for the hills!].

Due to low self-esteem they're incredibly fragile and sensitive. They dish it out but can't receive it.

Even the smallest critique is met with intense emotions. You can't tell em this tho: I'd say avoid em son.

Tho' the older narc has learned to control themselves outwardly, it's still going on inside honey.

THE SILENT TREATMENT [STONEWALLING]

These outbursts can range from raging to silent treatment stonewalling but it's all the same.

You may be wondering "what did I just do?" cuz it takes nothing to trigger their full fledged reacting.

Being passive-aggressive their behaviors allows em to get their point across with deniability of it all.

How to deal with these parasitic freeloaders without squashing your good nature: be mature.

How to deal with these manipulative life-sucking people: Number one: WATCH what they do.

Watch for the times when you served them. They're so sneaky this may have to be hindsight friend.

Was it an emotional pull? Remember it's all a performance with the narcissist, that's all.

BE ON THE WATCH ALWAYS

Pray for discernment as you watch their behavior for at getting what they want they are MASTERS.

NEVER AGAIN

As you watch carefully you'll see the leach. It's a real turnoff though it's so subtle as they speak.

The narc's goal at all times is to get you to serve them though they'll act like it's the opposite friend.

Whenever it was, they wanted something from you and masterfully got you to give it to them Sue.

On the outer they seem like good people even churchgoers--but it's all a performance sir.

Before your discernment is developed you'll fall for that but later on you'll wonder "how could I have?"

They aren't thankful for what they have, they only covet what you have so its irrelevant what you gave.

NARC TACTICS/YOUR REACTIONS

The narc's silent treatment is designed to punish and manipulate, creating anxiety and fear ok.

With that conflict survival takes precedence over the relationship, leading to trauma responses.

Major trauma: The narc's tactics aren't visible to outsiders, so the world think's they're nice.

Your trauma response is hypervigilance: while your world falls apart you get more nervous.

NO one on the outside understands what's going on behind closed doors: it's a hidden war.

This isolation makes it harder for the victim to recognize and address the issue [this is abusive too].

One is caught in a toxic cycle preventing control or freedom from the relationship: it's a bad trip.

NEVER AGAIN

Any relationship based on fear/intimidation is not from God but a terrifying cobweb in which we're caught.

God gives us peace, not control. It's a combat zone ruled by tactics like the silent treatment et. al.

Even the malignant narcissist [sociopath] lovebombs. That's an important point so don't take it on.

Don't be a masochist. There are people God wants you to walk away from, not endure though a mess.

WALK AWAY, NEVER ENDURE

Walk away: not endure with, not forebear under, not love on ok. But dismiss immediately today,

God doesn't want bad influences in your life. Those with bad intentions worm their way in, aye.

Don't "look for the good" in one who's infecting you demonically. It's all about spirits honey.

If they disrespect your values or manipulate for personal gain, that's a bad influence to get rid of ok.

If they're leading you down a path God has already delivered you from, make em leave hon'.

If this was someone you just met, would you let em in? Then what is forcing you to stay with em?

Don't say "maybe they're here for a reason" when the truth is you don't want the confrontation.

WHY ARE YOU KEEPING THEM?

If you're trying to fit a square peg in a round hole, ask WHY you're keeping them in your life at all.

NEVER AGAIN

Why stay in a relationship that is corrupting you? That is the lifesaving question so don't avoid it Sue.

It's not the lack of mistakes marking a good relationship but the quickness of repentance: that's it.

Paul said "drive out that sinner" and "hand him over to Satan" not be a doormat and be nice to him.

LOVEBOMBING OF PSYCHOPATHS

Even a psychopath will lovebomb you. So it depends on how codependent & susceptible you are too.

Narc abuse is pure confusion as they accuse you of what they do: ghost you then cry it's YOU.

She ghosted me out of envy then wrote "what can I do to return things to the how they were before?"

As Christians we wanna do the right thing so question ourselves as if we're the problem see.

She did a mean thing so you stopped communicating then she came back at you, whimpering.

Joseph's brothers were jealous of a coat his father gave him & they sold him into slavery for that friend.

We aren't called to bear under abuse! For that condemns the just & condones the wicked too.

The collateral damage from these situations can trickle down to later generations, so let it go son.

KEEP EM OUT ONCE GONE

If God has already removed someone from your life, you're gonna wanna keep em out, no lie.

NEVER AGAIN

God doesn't take us backwards. He doesn't lead us to a banquet of glory then dumpster dive on the way.

Once you go no-contact you discover the relationship was even more toxic than you thought!

Sometimes no-contact is exactly what you need to get the healing, for it's pure hell staying in the ring.

WONDERFUL RELIEF OF LETTING GO

You let go of the hurts, hopes & expectations when going no-contact. It's a wonderful relief in fact.

No-contact is a reality test. This person says this but then does THAT and is in fact an older brat.

For that duration you're not going to trust them and instead protect your heart in the interim.

It's a lot easier to just cut em off. Ask God if you should have those hard conversations about it all.

If you cut em off only to go back, you gotta go thru the process all over again and reality goes black.

It doesn't mean it won't hurt, just that you won't be operating from emotional drivers/triggers.

Keep your grass low to reveal snakes. You don't wanna be lovebombed again, pray for discernment ok.

You're too nice, vulnerable and gullible until you never take it again, then discernment is your friend.

FROM FITTING TO ESCAPING

GOD HATH RELOCATED ME
GOD'S GREAT PLAN BACK THEN
LOVE EM FROM A DISTANCE
YOU'VE COME TOO FAR FOR THIS
JEALOUSY FROM FAKE FAMILY
FOLLOW THE RULES & LAY LOW
MIND YOUR OWN, LIVE LONG
RELOCATE AND IT ALL CHANGES
THEY'RE MAD YOU DON'T ANSWER
LEAVE OR BECOME SALT: NOTHING
ALL FORMER THINGS PASS AWAY
YOU WERE THEIR ENERGY SOURCE
THE FUTURE IS INCREDIBLE
DON'T STOP THEIR KARMA
THEY DEMORALIZED YOUR DREAMS
JEALOUS FROM THE WOMB
IT'S FROM THE *INSIDE* OF YOU
STOP TRIPPIN' OVER KARMICS

FROM FITTING TO ESCAPING

GOD HATH RELOCATED ME

God had to relocate me, the persecution was that bad let alone the jealousy. 26 years of treachery.

I completed my season of treason and God took me from my cabin to a mansion, it was done.

God yanked me from toxic environment in the middle of the night. Instantly I was treated right.

It was my season of treason: I HAD to go thru it all. Heroes have canyons to overcome y'all.

I asked "WHY do I have to go thru this shit man?" and He said "you're destined for greatness", amen!

You gotta go thru it to get to it. Understand what I'm saying: it's an archetypal process: becoming.

God would never forsake you but He knows what you must go thru. You gotta get tougher Sue.

GOD'S GREAT PLAN BACK THEN

God's great plan: People bugged me so incessantly I wrote 98 books on Social Psychology see.

After living in a dusty cabin [and being grateful for that man] He put me in a safe/gorgeous mansion.

God will do the same for you. I guarantee if you'll persevere your sad situation you'll be saved too.

When God said "enough is enough" He planted my feet on higher ground and I escaped all that stuff.

FROM FITTING TO ESCAPING

I decree that new life and home will be yours in the name of Jesus, for you've paid the price.

Once God elevates you to the upper room there's nothing they can do to bring you down Sue

They have a playbook they'll keep using. When you do A they'll do B and nothing can change em see.

LOVE EM FROM A DISTANCE

Love em from a distance and don't get involved again sis. Get new friends and ask God for this.

They don't know how to act any other way so they'll do it again if you get hooked so stay the hell away.

When you unhooked from them God gave you all these blessings. Enjoy them & don't ever go back in.

When you stopped involvement God took it the rest of the way. Now don't go back or you'll fall ok.

Give it time, they'll show you who they really are. With that red flag, go ghost and become a star.

Remove yourself in a heartbeat. You're now gone like they never existed, that's how to do it see.

YOU'VE COME TOO FAR FOR THIS

You've come too far and done too much. You've got too much to lose to get re-involved with that bunch.

Once a chosen is fed up, there's nothing anyone can do about it. Sounds like the narc doesn't it kid.

Once you see they're holding you down, be gone. Go your separate ways and bid em well, that's all.

FROM FITTING TO ESCAPING

When with them you started to put them first, forgetting about God. That's inevitable with the flawed.

"You put these backstabbers before me, when I took you from rock bottom?" You won't blossom.

Your success brought a lot of hate from the enemy so you can't play around and ever go back see.

JEALOUSY FROM FAKE FAMILY

Envy/jealousy came from your own family and friends so you gotta go ghost to stay on top, amen.

You can't take all their toxic energy while trying to go to the next level. Recall that always: skirt the devil.

You guys are not the same so you must never give in. The devil says you're lonely but ignore him.

The devil is a liar. Every time you take them back they'll set you back but standing firm you'll go higher.

You keep pressing higher to your high calling in Jesus, and let em feel the impact of your absence.

If they didn't appreciate your presence they deserve your absence and nothing will change that sis.

Your nosy neighbors hate the fact you're private. They're watching every move when you make it.

FOLLOW THE RULES & LAY LOW

Follow the rules, pay your rent and go on with your business. Be lowkey and lock the door sis.

If you're paying your bills, don't give a dam. You gotta pay the cost to be boss and that's all man.

FROM FITTING TO ESCAPING

They hate it when you're harmless as a dove but wise as a serpent: when they can't find anything darnit.

As chosens we're really good neighbors but we don't let anyone close mixing business with pleasure.

Let's make a pact: none of us will go back. Chosens are rare and a giant success if staying alone: fact.

MIND YOUR OWN, LIVE LONG

If you mind your own, you live long. Keep em at an arm's distance and you'll be fine [keep music down].

You got nosy neighbors then shifty ones. Whatever, the chosens are low key, that's how they run.

Be pleasant & respectful but keep it moving. That's how you live as a chosen in this era so draining.

Your home shows sanity and peace of mind. That's where you can rest so stay separate, be fine.

Nevertheless, pray over all of them because this is where you stay. Home is precious/sacred ok?

When I was trying to find myself it was about fitting in when God was calling me to leave em.

I couldn't stand it when they'd drop by. That was a sign God hated it too so He yanked me out, aye.

RELOCATE AND IT ALL CHANGES

When I relocated everything changed. Not just people but drinking, drugging and all partying ok.

I was so vulnerable thinking I could trust friends and family. What a shock when I learned finally.

FROM FITTING TO ESCAPING

The more I kept going back in trust the worse it got until I hit bottom on all of it and just trusted God.

As you grow up in the fear/admonition of God [escaping all] they will hate you, wishing you to fall.

Some will hate you for never being the same again. The herd wants the status quo, it's all built in.

THEY'RE MAD YOU DON'T ANSWER

They're mad you won't answer the phone now or respond to texts. Proceed on this path ok sis?

Since you left it all behind God's voice is clear & resonant in your mind and success is here, aye.

Their evil spirits are calling & it's tempting but listen to me: persevere on escaping & you'll be winning.

From hate to begging you back, they respond in cycles: "what happened? What must I do to now?""

You're so used to bad events it's hard to realize you're now in a winning process but don't relent!

They're so empty, since you left everything fell apart in their lives. So they beg, cry, get angry: aye!

Your absence is felt in a hate-love combo. They hate you for leaving but that's the way it is ya know.

LEAVE OR BECOME SALT: NOTHING

If you hadn't left them behind you'd be a pillar of salt: NOTHING. But you took that step, fortunately.

You made the same decision Lot made. He said "I'm getting the hell outa here!" and he was saved.

FROM FITTING TO ESCAPING

Lot told family "come with me" and they didn't want to see: that's how it always is when you leave.

You tried to help em. You told them your vision & they laughed, didn't they friend? It's too late, amen.

They didn't believe you then but believe you now. Cuz they're watching you win but too late: wow!

ALL FORMER THINGS PASS AWAY

They watch you become successful [the next big thing] as all former things are passed away see.

You've got your health back. Your strength, you're glow and energy: you've de-aged into beauty: fact.

You are beautifully, wonderfully and fearfully made in the likeness and image of God, no flaws.

Your praying nights and daily fastings did it. Not going back in revenge really paid off didn't it?

They'll be going thru karma for the rest of their lives for what they did to you. That is real life Sue.

They're shocked cuz they can't get easy access to your energy anymore but I'm sorry, there's the door.

YOU WERE THEIR ENERGY SOURCE

You were the energy source to the family, you were their provider but they mocked you as a grasshopper.

You were sent to bless those people but they ruined it. Yet they ain't seen nothing yet, just expect it.

Acknowledging you destroys their ego. It's a very painful thing to grow up and let that go.

FROM FITTING TO ESCAPING

Since you saw who they were you don't respond to texts anymore and they are mad, hitting the floor.

They flip between begging you back and being angry and vindictive so beware of these sad sacks.

After going through all that, just look forward to total world success now and winning after combat.

THE FUTURE IS INCREDIBLE

It's going to be so incredible with all the perks. You'll gain mass attractions and love, not jerks.

God will take you from your dusty cabin to a mansion and for all the acclaim & fame it'll be amazin'.

Hurray, your time has finally come. What you've been waiting for and visualizing when put down.

Your enemy **WILL** lovebomb you because they're already shown they'll do anything to accrue.

This is your winning season after going thru hell with friends & family's treason so enjoy it son.

If you don't feel they deserve it think of all God saw behind the scenes and you'll understand it.

You're such a good person you wanna forgive & forget all they've been doin' but God vindicates, let Him.

As you see the seasons changing with you **UP** and them **DOWN** let it all happen and that's all son.

DON'T STOP THEIR KARMA

God says don't stop their punishment or bad vibes will come back on you: let Him handle it Sue.

FROM FITTING TO ESCAPING

They chose those who were richer/more popular over you. Reject those too, part of the worldly/cruel.

They've been jealous from the beginning and that's why you never got the support you're needing.

They never acknowledged you in your presence cuz it destroyed their ego/sense of entitlement.

THEY DEMORALIZED YOUR DREAMS

They demoralized your dreams and self-esteem, saying you'd never be the next big thing it seems.

You had emotional damage over those not supporting you, taking years to get to here cuza that too.

You have secret admirers out here so forget those who'd never support you out of ego, pride or fear.

NO ONE ever came to save you. There was only Jesus and His angels so remember that always Sue.

They don't have to acknowledge you cuz God's ready to publicly honor you right in their face Sue.

You did everything together and suddenly they lashed out in jealousy and envy. It just came out see.

When God gave you just a sprinklin' of the blessin' they came at you foul, gossipin' and hatin'.

JEALOUS FROM THE WOMB

They've been jealous of you from the womb it's just now coming out to the light. It's a spiritual blight.

God's trying to tell you these are not your people. He's trying to save you from that herd of evil.

FROM FITTING TO ESCAPING

If it hadn't been for the Lord these people woulda destroyed us long ago, the Psalms says so.

You've been wondering why you're by yourself. The higher you climb the smaller your circle elf.

They can't support you nor themselves. They self-medicate feeling so small in nothingness.

IT'S FROM THE *INSIDE* OF YOU

What they don't understand is it's on the INSIDE of you. It's was a spiritual battle from the beginning Sue.

Now free God will send you people on the same level and they'll help you get to the next plateau.

You expected people to support you who weren't even healed. You were one with forces out of keel.

How would those people know how to honor greatness? You were blocked by mediocrity your highness.

You'll get more support from the average Joe on the street who NEEDS what you're saying see.

You don't need anyone's support. God is your catalyst and cushion to rely on so hearken to the Lord.

STOP TRIPPIN' OVER KARMICS

Stop tripping over karmics & fake family members. They NEVER cared & you've suffered enough sister.

Declutter your phone cuz half of em aren't going to the next level with you and are better off gone.

Don't be a fool: if you were in the hospital half of your contact list wouldn't even come to see you.

HAZE OF
LATTER DAYS

HAZE OF
LATTER DAYS

HAZE OF LATTER DAYS

Satan's Crowd is Loud but
We Made it outa the Game

I'M NOT AN EXTROVERT

I'm not an extrovert and I hate social occasions but I realize it's not necessary for salvation.

I don't care that you can explain it [early trauma] I can't stand it and don't want it in my house.

Tho' damaged as children we are still responsible for our actions like any hurt/harassed heathen.

I was never socialized. My only social stance is to be above em all while being sweet and cordial.

It's abundantly clear, absurdly evident/not up for debate: democrats are the hypocrites of hate.

A gangrape victim of ten men was still shaking and crying 20 years later--PTSD from the worst torture.

It wasn't Jane or Mary but the whole liberal feminist narrative coming thru women generally.

Our tank can only go so low. If not getting back what we're giving we lose ourselves ya know?

HATE AFFECTS US PSYCHOLOGICALLY

To be hated affects one psychologically. It makes one nuts and ironically collapses boundaries.

HAZE OF THE LATTER DAYS

The narcissist needs you, to be converted to the bad object absorbing his toxic waste constantly.

He's constantly onto external objects to convert them to bad so he can offload all this crap.

He imbues the external object with toxicity and relates only to "it" as a garbage dumping ground.

Then you become the culprit and him the victim so he avoids you--the characteristic ghosting.

Why do they hate Donald Trump? Haters gonna hate--they hated Jesus Christ just as much.

Some are hated from the moment of birth--that alone shows their exalted origins, not a curse.

I WAS JEALOUS OF SOCIAL PEOPLE

I was jealous of social people all my life cuz they fit and I didn't--they were mellow but I felt strife.

Now I see they're just part of the herd, something I want none of, and separation was holy enough.

All the time: distractions, interruptions, ringing phones, barking dogs. Leave me alone/cover me God.

Once scapegoat leaves persecuting family system they all shrivel to nothing-- they NEED him.

Since kindergarten I was jealous of & felt inferior to those who could fit in--our gregarious friends.

I wasn't intentionally different-I just was. They were never my concern but I felt hurt at their rebuff.

Now I see those who can pass go are the hypnotized socials and I'm no longer envious at all.

HAZE OF THE LATTER DAYS

It was when Mr./Mrs. Social Charm were chosen as deacons in the church that I made the switch.

FEMALE FUNCTION

I would be behind you forever, I would further your work and open your mind to a phantasmagoria.

That's the female's function: to open up the portals of their minds. To spur them on, to be kind.

A female teacher opens a boy up to his destiny--a first love, a counselor, your sister--whatever.

If not his mother, a woman appears somewhere and he changes, sparking creative arrangements.

I couldn't adapt to such mediocrity. It was all so silly, it was boring as hell, I wanted to go home see.

INDIVIDUAL SUPERIOR TO THE GROUP

Individual is always superior to the group--all thru history this is true. Going solo is for the genius few.

If the female is immoral she can't spark changes. Women: be holy so God can change your charges.

You sent him not just a picture but an ARCHETYPE which tells worlds of wisdom not just the hype.

Archetypal Psychiatry: see the fools. The world is seen thru the archetypes/the low are like cartoons.

Fall into a new archetypal strata and your whole world changes--now a wonderful fantasy not hellish.

Philosopher, poet, psychologist, theoretician, playwright, home creator and mostly happy housewife.

HAZE OF THE LATTER DAYS

When I'm with em they are SO SLOW. I'm light years ahead at a different steam pressure: GO.

They look me up and down, the women hate me and are suspicious.: the fun party of the hellish.

The snide remark you made hitting like a bomb while I was poised nevertheless: good riddance!

The social world is marked by "polite cruelties." They're so subtle you must stay alert to fortify thee.

NON-VERBAL COMMUNICATION

85% of communication is NON-verbal. Just a raised eyebrow is enough to put em down/tell all.

I walk into a room of em and pick up on the whole bagashit. It hurts on deep levels/I'm done with it.

What they put me thru--those hardass feminists agreeing to evil stuff--was inconceivable/horrendous.

And here she evolves to the comportment of a queen: Aristocratic reserve, being above but kind.

They hung together and squeezed me out, it was always two against one--emotional suffocation.

No matter what I said or did it didn't matter at all. They were closed/stubborn/obdurate as hell.

Women are so pathologically jealous it's in their DNA. But in evil periods it explodes like we see today.

Stay alone for awhile, go at your own steam pressure and you'll find they are SO SLOW and immature.

I was so bored in every group. It's the lowest common denominator, an anti-genius force: pooh!

HAZE OF THE LATTER DAYS

Way to deal with intrusive men: Be a little lady and the other men will defend you against him.

But if you're immoral no man will defend you, he'll even throw you to the wolves you foolishly let in.

I felt imprisoned in a shell/wanted to burst out but afraid of their reactions--I'm whole only now.

That explains the system: people are controlled by other's reactions not inner divine guidance.

My growing up, the biggest sign: I'm no longer jealous of Mrs. Social Charm/virtue-signaling swine.

A phony social manipulator taking over EVERY situation with her shrewd & cunning balance of forces.

Continually balancing forces with her on top, constantly manipulating people usually with gossip.

I'd never go back into that evil chicken coop of hens going for recognition using their image magic.

POPULARITY DOESN'T MATTER

Insight: it doesn't matter if it's popular or not. Stop gauging things by what they like, it's all rot.

Balancing forces: One gets too big, she undercuts them or puts another up. That's her life nonstop.

It's homeostasis: in systems water seeks it's own level. Get too high, get insults--too low, pep talks.

It's like we spoke a different language. I was a stranger in a strange land and it was terrifying/strange.

Remember this: things are never as bad as they seem to you, a victim of scary nights and PTSD.

HAZE OF THE LATTER DAYS

It's like we spoke a different language. I was a stranger in a strange land and it was a terrifying phase.

The only way to adapt is to mal-adapt by giving up personal reality totally, but self is healer see.

You remember the incident best, they've forgotten long ago or it's faded into vacuity with the rest.

There was never any real memories just magnetisms of the moment which change as we grow up.

It's not the **EVENT** which is remembered but the other's reactions **TO** it and it helps to know that.

The superior's reactions determine how we see events but that too all changes with disrespect.

How we see ourselves is determined by the ground but with disrespect the true self illumines quick.

It was Interactional Dysynchrony: when comfortable interaction becomes awkward suddenly.

I'm an introvert who hates social occasions but you're telling me it's a requirement for salvation?

As long as you didn't have sex you can be happy with the reject but if you did it's a terrible hex.

You're filled with shame and remorse but they don't even remember it or it's vaporized with the dross.

He likes opera a lot but I like boom-boom rap [heavy on the lower end] because I'm Black Scot.

Without a man to protect me I'm a sitting duck but feminists say we're best alone, good luck.

AGEISM: SEEING AGE AS DISEASE

HAZE OF THE LATTER DAYS

They see age as a disease. A source of embarrassment and disappointment being obsolete.

Just when you're at the apex of life, the top of your game and best at your trade you're seen as lame.

I know you love phase one--sex/love chemicals--but for true relationship you lack skill sets ya' know.

The callous and brazen things you say make me avoid your whole generation cuz they're crazy.

I'm protected in a castle with a molt now but how I'd adapt if back in the herd again, I don't know.

It's a severe undertow in the herd, you lose your mind and forget or subsume all that YOU preferred.

LOVEBOMBING THIRST

If lovebombing works you've probably a love thirst from an early trauma and attachment curse.

Don't assiduously work, instead DON'T work then let the subconscious brings up all the words.

You've grown into a whole new universe. Most likely you can't relate to anyone you knew previous.

It takes more drive to non-work than work but it's very productive to take a nap or a nice walk.

Public schools messed up my mind and I didn't know it. Many people went crazy acting out then blew it.

If you stand up for yourself or the values of our country the mob will try to destroy you, count on it.

When I stood up for my privacy they tried to destroy me. Any sign of independence was their enemy.

HAZE OF THE LATTER DAYS

The pathologically regressive atmosphere of the university made me crazy as I mal-adapted to insanity.

JUSTICE: They were intrusive, dogmatic, accusatory, belittling, wrong, secular/sexual, stereotypic.

They threw paper airplanes for not saying "he & she" rather than "he" the nonpersonal pronoun used thru history.

They bully you into adapting to their current narrative even though no one ever thought it until yesterday.

You've let the brats get away with crap for 90 days so they're compelled to push boundaries.

IT'S ABOUT WHO OWNS REALITY

It no longer matters what truth is, it's who owns reality. They own it now and are defining it daily.

Their drive in life is not for home/family and God but evil: the flaccid praise of other empty people.

Like peas in a pod, they're perfectly fitting then there's you: misfit black sheep destined to be great.

They suck up and spit down. And if you get in their way they will punish you and ruin your rep in town.

There's a totalitarian takeover of the left in this era. Total means everything: words and thoughts.

You don't believe their crap--their liberal narrative learned in college--so they wanna destroy your rep.

Left-wing activists disguised as journalists fabricate a new reality that no one takes seriously.

The don't want to have a conversation with you they want to destroy you. Society now is only groups.

HAZE OF THE LATTER DAYS

Chatting it up: It's actually flirting it up as he gets real close to her face, moving in non-stop.

Being smart, deep and articulate dates you. You're a dam dinosaur if you wanna look deeply into.

REMORSE AND CENSURSHIP

You spend the second half of life getting over the first half. That's the way it is so learn to laugh.

We're coming into a new era where we can't say anything and I've said enough already, that's the thing.

Coming back from college with contumacy: griping at parents and bringing it ALL up you see.

It's when they come back from college that all hell breaks loose. It's an alien matrix you don't choose.

Making it a moral issue that you agree with them and shunning you with disdain if you do not.

Not only disdain or even disgust but horror that you don't go along with this crap/globalist scam.

Narcissists: It's not so much they love themselves but they can't get past themselves/traumatized.

NARCISSISTS BUST BOUNDARIES

The narcissist actually perceives your boundary-setting as aggression and sadistic humiliation.

He shit-tests you to see what you can take as the Good Mother--re-enacting early conflicts more.

Rules for clown world: Masks doesn't work, wear it. Vaccine doesn't work, take it. Alex Jones

HAZE OF THE LATTER DAYS

Monster chicken-necked control freaks, vicious gossips/haters called "ladies you should meet".

God took my side even when at my worst--it was like He didn't see it/wiped it out so I'd come first.

God was my Champion cuz He chose me and I was irresistibly pulled to Him despite my sins.

How to rise up in your field as Number One: completely withdraw from the human herd right now.

Yes I'm emphatic but I get so tired of the loquacious folderol I have to cut thru it somehow.

My superior friend said "you've let too many people into your life" and I never saw him again: lesson.

It feels like I have a tidal wave inside that was suppressed and I'm about to burst but God leads first.

Answer to acid reflux: one meal a day, low glycation. Answer to choking: no solid food again.

Only way to cut thru loquacious folderol is with terseness, logic quick, laconic wit, be ready for it.

Carb up: grape juice and cliff bar at 5 am. It energizes me so I won't lie down and choke again.

Seems like such a quiet neighborhood but get involved with any party and you're shafted for good.

The feminine instincts reversed become the cruelest. Understanding inversion this makes sense.

An evil freak is deformed thru sin. He doesn't give a dam about you or me cuz Satan runs the engine.

ELDERING IS HIGHEST CONSCIOUSNESS

HAZE OF THE LATTER DAYS

Not one fowl word: 1949 movies were beautiful, perfected, detailed, deep, never hear a curse.

In young women beauty's an accident but in older women it's an achievement and you've got it.

Eldering is when you leave the world behind man. No more petty competitions/trying to fit in.

In eldering you're finally a Unique Self. That's what God wants: peculiar treasures/magic elves.

Eldering is like slipping on cozy pajamas. No more trying to fit in you're just yourself/your only drama.

You'll be fine if you don't mix in too much. Maintain your integrity, separate as such--that's my hunch.

Iron sharpens iron. It's good to confront a challenge, debate makes you look prepared/managed.

I partied so much I needed a crutch. I had to scale it back so chose instead to study/write a bunch.

NARCISSISTS ARE FICKLE

Narcissists are a bit fickle. You go from a fairytale of love bombing to an ex horror story of a sicko.

Whether it happens overnight or in a slow subtle transition it's a nightmare/you miss him.

Their goal is to make you fall in love with the IDEA of who they SEEM to be, relaxing all your boundaries.

You love him, he knows you do, and that's when the devaluation phase takes place in the stew.

Devaluation phase: really cruel jokes ["just kidding"] and trying to make you jealous with other women.

HAZE OF THE LATTER DAYS

It means blows to your self-esteem, hits to your ego, who you are as a person, triangulation/jealousy.

You're devalued when he gets bored. He loves the love bombing chemicals but in phase 2 discards.

When the new car smell wears off narcissists have the attention span of a moth and they say "goeth".

You adore them and they love it but after a month you're not giving a huge ego boost/they resent it.

You can't get enough of them at first but after months things return to "normal" and you're cursed.

NARCISSISTIC DEPEDESTABLIZATION

It's when you move from the honeymoon to something more stable and mature that this appears.

When the romance is dead and it doesn't last long they switch out to drama and joy goes way down.

Here they had you on a pedestal of exalted perfection and now see you are flawed, imperfect, human.

Now you're someone they didn't realize you were. They feel cheated, they are being mistreated.

However you wanna say it, you appeared to be one way but deceived. They were duped/cheated.

They get resentful, mean, cold and cruel. Now they monkey-branch to find another like you.

At this point they find another one who's "perfect" before they discard you, the imminent reject.

Why do they pull back hot and cold? This is essentially the reason: they're looking for another doll.

HAZE OF THE LATTER DAYS

A narcissist is like a fisherman. He always has ten rods around his boat waiting for something to happen.

NARCISSISTIC FISHING

A narcissist is like a fisherman, with ten lines around his boat waiting for something to happen.

He always has a line in the water and once you object he's instantly on the lookout for another sucker.

If not a reject you'll be put on the bench and wait to be hoovered and for some this lasts years.

As you're waiting and praying to be hoovered he's done with you sister but may not say it at first.

If you figure this out and speak to them about it you'll be devalued again and then frustrated over it.

If there's a break in the relationship and you go back the sequence is quicker: devalued far sooner.

Triangulation and jealousy are big in his devaluation. He needs you to have fear in your heart hon'

They need you to be jealous of others or you might leave but a high value woman does it immediately.

PUBLIC FLIRTING WITH STRANGERS

When he blatantly and publicly flirts, your reaction is his current supply and he needs it tho' you cry.

Insults: ugly, fat, poor, useless, old, a turnoff. You feel nervous, unhappy, obsolete, brushed off.

Hey: if he's running cold with you he's running hot with someone else. Don't doubt me on that elf.

HAZE OF THE LATTER DAYS

When he grows cold you step your game up, the mark of a female chump—walk away, give up.

You may try harder to make them happy but in the end it never works anyway, it's their pattern see.

A lady makes up her mind to NEVER, EVER be on the begging end with men. Melania Trump

You don't beg him to spend more time/stay with you. To a real man could anything be more disgusting?

A lady never chases a man. Make him know you're alive then go on with YOUR life, that's attraction.

Never beg him to stay/spend more time with you. To a real man with a life you seem like a fool.

I don't give thought to a man who doesn't love and put me first, and none other. Melania Trump

Your love bombing gave him an ego boost. But in the devaluing stage you chased, begged, fussed.

Don't let him hoover you back when he feels like it. He's got a lull in his action--that's all--so forget it.

PEOPLE ARE THE PROBLEM

The only way I'm totally happy with my neighbors is to not go to any of their social functions ever.

I never once complained that you don't listen/talk right thru me but honey we gotta live separately.

They can do the first phase of lovebombing--anyone can--but not later phases of consistency/stability.

It's ok to be different but not if you're drunk once in awhile and other bad lifestyles of the defiled.

HAZE OF THE LATTER DAYS

If you're gonna be different better be moral too cuz due to differences they're perched to get you.

Being different--divinely peculiar, unique--will never fly if you're a drunk, a slut or anything like that.

Repentance gives your speech boldness. I couldn't talk about drunks/sluts if I were still one Miss.

What distinguishes the saints is their unheard of courage [BOLDNESS] in public--could you do it?

EVERY HERD HAS HOMEOSTASIS

A huge resistance to anyone outa step with the herd they're in--that's where strength comes in.

Strength to be unique is not muscular but spiritual, from repentance from these sins known to us all.

As Jung said, for every sin there is a seed of compensation in the present--you SHOW it.

Every herd has different reactions to unique differences and some are downright Commie conformist.

I couldn't understand why the women hated me but now I know: they're the biggest conformists see.

The female community punishes unique differences and its a cruel thing to be the odd girl out see.

The biggest obstruction to female genius is **NOT** men but the female community.

Stop smiling like a Cheshire cat in pictures. It looks ridiculous, you should be serious, it's social sickness.

You think war victims are smiling like that? It's fake, not at all natural--and bearing teeth says FIGHT.

HAZE OF THE LATTER DAYS

I was terrified in kindergarten being told to love my neighbors. They were crazy, evil, robbers.

THE SOCIAL GENERATION SUX

I hated the social expectations and stayed alone the whole time. I wanted to become sublime.

I couldn't stand it when they'd bring their friends--but that's the socials, they never question it.

I couldn't stand my peers all thru school. Mean, ruthless, unruly, gossipy, treacherous, untrustworthy.

That's who they were but of course it was all covered over with a veneer--high profile acceptable peers.

So presumptuous, imposing people on me without me ever vetting--that's liberal California I guess.

I would lay a boundary and they'd instantly bust it cuz the social world is fusion without separation.

Would this other guy--greener pastures--come thru for you when things really suck? Think of that.

It is horrifying to be the black sheep destined to be great while in the chicken coop of status grades.

They wanna see you as inferior so they can project all their crap onto you, the scapegoat.

They can't bear to see you as superior, and you're sure not on their level, so they peg you down.

IDENTITY STRUGGLES AND PROJECTIONS

All of life is an identity struggle like this. When it happens in families, oh boy it gets destructive sis.

HAZE OF THE LATTER DAYS

All they could see was their own projections, not ME. And i knew it--just had to wait to outlive em see.

I know what persecution is like cuz I lived in a small desert town of liberals severely dumbed down.

When people don't understand you--when you don't fit their perceptions--they see you as subhuman.

It was always two against one, triangulation. They wouldn't listen, they had their projection.

Yes I went crazy but it was in reaction to this personal persecution of the socials against one.

I got a wod of cash and made it outa Borrego into a mansion with a gate: finally free of gall.

There is nothing like geographic relocation, a chance to completely start again, free of people/sins.

In an instant I was free of all those interactions which will never occur again, it was just an era I was in.

It's like snapping a chord and suddenly you're in a new dimension, a balloon rising away from bedlam.

There's a certain low character person that gets even meaner in victory. Pelosi shows this also AOC.

CENSURESHIP IS "HARM REDUCTION"

It's not censorship it's "harm reduction". Reducing a liar's reach is different from censoring speech.

New York Times covered for Hitler and now they're calling for shutting down Fox news? It's unreal.

When did cancel culture get so ideological? Easy--they're the grandchildren of the hippies that's all.

HAZE OF THE LATTER DAYS

When she got back from college she ruined my life. I couldn't be who I was, she laid a trip on me.

They're mean from being filled with guilt from cheating massively and not deserving victory.

Their success is based on dishonesty and cannot stand. They'll pull themselves down as inferior men.

"Controversial and derogatory social media posts" is how they label those studying history/man's foes.

Political correctness implies a double standard by definition--all taboo codes do friends.

WHAT IS A WISE WOMAN?

ERASE SHAME by depedestalizing the shamer. It works instantly and like a miracle.

The wise woman builds her house but the fool pulls it down with her hands. Prov 14: 1

70% of divorces are initiated by women. They destroy the lives of their kids, PETS--everyone!

A faithful witness does not lie but a false witness always utters lies--that was my sisters as I cried.

The elder increases in intelligence as his temporal lobes burst open to reveal eternity--not less.

A scoffer just stays dumb but wisdom/knowledge is easy to him who understands. Proverbs 14: 6

The folly of fools is deceit. No wonder the victims go crazy as they respond to false accusations of the elite.

Fools and losers mock at sin but with the upright there is great favor as God situates them higher.

HAZE OF THE LATTER DAYS

The heart knows it's own bitterness/a stranger doesn't know your joy so keep things to yourself or annoy.

HOUSE OF THE WICKED

The house of the wicked is overthrown but the tent of the upright will flourish. It's happening, I attest to this.

Though his way seems right to a man it ends in death. His laughter is really sorrow/the end of mirth is grief.

The backslider is filled with his own ways but a good man is satisfied from above. Prov 14: 14

The simple believes every word [gullibility] but the prudent considers wisely every step [invincibility].

The raging fool is self-confident but a wise man FEARS and departs from evil while remaining humble.

A man of wicked intentions is hated and a quick-tempered man acts foolishly [prov. 14: 17] so shut up honey.

The simple inherit folly but the prudent are crowned with knowledge--chips off the ol' block: good parents.

Evil bows before good/the wicked at gates of the righteous but to get here we had to go through much.

The poor is hated even by his own neighbor but the rich have many friends-- isn't that the truth sir.

CHATTER LEADS TO POVERTY

In all labor there is profit but idle chatter leads to poverty so PLEASE, I'm begging you: just shut up.

When the cops left lunacy filled the void. This is obvious to clear minds but to the left we're just paranoid.

HAZE OF THE LATTER DAYS

You're less guilty of sin than collapsed boundaries--the hedge was down so evil flowed in suddenly.

Put a smile on knowing God wants us to be happy. Not somber but sober, not maudlin but grateful for.

When do you get to your throne? When strong enough to keep everyone else away: your spiritual home.

Trauma brings a restructuring of the brain and I'll never be the same. I'm at a much higher place, just sayin'

Just one screw loose and she became a drunken slut and kleptomaniac. The whole mess, just forget it.

You work all your life for applause of the crowd and when it's over in a minute then what? Only God.

Aging is not the wearing out of parts but the completion of more meaningful wholes, and what a role.

Women in politix are either best or worst. When they take over watch out whether state or coffee klatsch.

Old people can be the best or the worst. Fine elegant elderly gentleman or dirty old man: you choose.

ORAL SEX AND DEGRADING PASSIONS

Your mouth was not made for that. Ever since Deep Throat in 70's women were debased by those dirty rats.

It's not a matter of your time running out for God will surely pack in your latter days, every moment ablaze.

Bible calls em "degrading passions". It's disgusting and a true lady's not having it despite the resistance.

If you give into the degrading passions of men you're a dam fool and will be treated that way: cruel.

HAZE OF THE LATTER DAYS

Ever since Deep Throat women expected to debase themselves that way and the dirty thing's not ok.

Expected to act lower than animals, to go along with every new perversion and then tell everyone.

People didn't use to act like this, there was mutual respect between partners vs. Perverse Postmoderns.

The main reason they're all zombies is the sex perversions you're not seein' and they see as achievement.

Degrading Practices. First it was Deep Throat and then it was Bill Clinton in is office that started all this.

WOMEN RAILROADED INTO IT

Ever since then women were expected to lest there'd be a Monica Lewinsky her husband would turn to.

The prevalence of oral sex means everyone is sick and demon possessed. That's the truth sis.

The whole generation is warped so there must be a moral revolution to revert us back to what God rewards.

It was Deep Throat in the seventies and then Bill Clinton who influenced what was expected of women.

Friends with benefits is the most disgusting thing yet. It doesn't matter if it's mutual you dirty old coot.

Are you still clinging to someone you deplore? Cuz that's how it works as self-esteem falls to the floor.

I'm gonna depedestalize you today. I'm gonna peel you away because you're not right within, ok?

BILL CLINTON DETERMINED DESTINY

HAZE OF THE LATTER DAYS

Due to Deep Throat and then Bill Clinton American men have been degrading their women for decades.

To even ASK for such a thing is so arrogant, devilish, abusive, selfish, whorish--such men are pigs.

If a man asks for that he wants to DEGRADE the woman! This is inexcusable and disgusting as well!

Any woman who would do such a thing has already agreed to her degradation to worm status and he hates ya.

The men have RAILROADED the women to do this--even on a regular basis! Saying "it's the in thing" miss.

Something about mass expectations of something--it's condemns dissidents from that line of thinking.

We've been made to accept pansexuality--ALL things go--but they do NOT: There are lines sweetie.

Oh my, if someone doesn't have parental guidance--way out there copying rats trying to destroy us.

Ok so that's not my thing--will that make him go to a Monica Lewinsky ya' think?

HUMILITY AND SUCCESS

The superior man is humble in his success cuz he knows how fast he can lose it and it's his last chance.

The narcissist doesn't know why he does it. He just needs to make you jealous, put you in your place, etc.

Once done with all details you can party all day long and night too. Celebrate achievements/mind cruise.

You can be as arrogant/conceited as you please if your motives are good. You've achieved it all.

HAZE OF THE LATTER DAYS

DIFFICULT WOMEN VALUE TIME

To him she's "difficult" because she has self-esteem, likes herself and sees her time as valuable.

To be that angry, and to have it all dissolve in a minute just from forgiving mom or another's insanity--wowie.

The therapist asked if I loved myself and I said I must--I'm the only one I wanna be with all the time or most.

The narcissist talks in mixed word salad as his actions seek only to make jealous, put in place. say who's bad.

I'm sayin' some third rate movie in the seventies and Bill Clinton actually determined our sexual destiny.

That era reminds me of some weird tantra statue in India with a 100 people sexually entangled--it is evil.

Where's the line, or is there to be NO line? Shouldn't this be discussed or just give in to self-disgust?

The narcissist approval-seeker is a sponge of his generation and it can get really bad son.

Sure they were always doing it but the bellshaped curve was still decent folk not this continuous orgy.

Through gradual acclimation to the [lower sensual] level it is approved by the social then we enter hell.

There's too much repetition/overstressing irrelevant points and I get it, I GET it but must turn you off.

Think of it: the president of the United States normalized perversion and then it was expected of all women.

You made it thru the war and now you're enjoying peace time--that's how to look at it. It's over, forget it.

POLITICS OF INTERACTION

What is Poli-Psych? The politics of interaction: who's superior to who determines who gets er dun.

You gotta draw a line somewhere and you have definitely crossed that line so get out foe of mine.

Having a sense of urgency indicates white supremacy? Yah we get er dun and progress very quickly.

The seasons have changed and that's a chance for a shift in the human life as well--you'll be amazed.

DEMOCRATS AND GLOBALISTS

Red Pill: George Soros is an unrepentant Nazi and he runs the entire show in most countries.

The same people saying cancel culture doesn't exist use it at every opportunity for a dystopian future.

The nightmare is hordes of ideological Jihadists who wield the power to banish nonconformists.

Hitlerian: we are deplatformed and silenced to the fringes of society with our reputations destroyed.

It's a slow process with globalists and Trump was a speedbump in what they want accomplished.

Now that Trump's out it's full speed ahead and thus we're experiencing all this tyranny and death.

Democrats are given a free pass to denigrate our laws, defame cops, excuse rioters, cheer mobs.

The reality of illegal immigration is: if we don't control/break it open we start being like them.

HAZE OF THE LATTER DAYS

Liberal underpinning goes by many names, all scary: wokism, cancel culture, critical race theory.

All these leftist modalities show a yearning for utopia and a disappointment with civilization.

It has a religious quality to it, a well-laid out cosmology: "we're all one" --all cliches so good-sounding.

The religious quality tho' false makes these ideas long-lasting and what a taint on civilization.

ADDENDUM

I'm not ashamed, I'm no communist. For a movie star or a famous author this would be a modest house.

Take care of elderly. They become weak tho' otherworldly near the end-- conduit to the cosmos.

The root issue is sin and always has been. God wanted to save us and the world from it's destruction.

Thank you enemy duds, you gave me so much to write about in 130 books on human chumps.

I pray God will reward you for all your work and that you'll be able to handle it with equanimity.

If your work is worth millions/if you've worked decades without a paycheck I pray God pays you today.

It takes all my might not to work. To hold back, not write, take a walk, listen music--work comes first.

All I can do is write, keep house, take care of pets and think. Other than that it's all music.

A well-ordered environment will expand your personality as a safe place to unfold, then it reflects it.

HAZE OF THE LATTER DAYS

We got outa California and Borrego just in time. Liberals were bombing our mailbox and other signs.

I know I was crazy, I know I did wrong but it was a friggin' demon which is also in them, so I forgive em.

He sent His Son who's our Best Friend, Brother, Husband & Champion when no one gives a dam.

The warmest hat ever is a French wool derby--beanies and too porous and do not compare see.

I will honor and take care of you and be your helpmate too--that's what a wife is supposed to do.

KK PICTURESTRIP

HAZE OF THE LATTER DAYS

The biggest impediment to the Trump agenda is establishment Republicans. Laura Ingraham

Must parrot the progressive consensus or lose it all (it's expensive).

If you express a conservative opinion, you'll be put on a black list and made an unemployable minion.

I can't abide any thought other than my own. SJW worldview

Let no one cheat you of your reward, taking delight in false humility or worshipping angels.

No wonder they accept weirdness and badness look at Harry Potter queerness and madness.

Queerness is a sign of the latter days. It always explodes in societies going down in a haze.

Music is not my art, it's a part of my life and life is my art. K.D. Lang

All he does is react to gossip/rumors (fake news) rather than just forging ahead in speed cruise.

Just stay the heck away. They're so gross and unrefined you could never explain so just escape!

When men were strong and did what's right, you didn't have this cuz blacks protected kids and wife.

German masochism comes from Nazi guilt drummed in for 3 generations since Europe was rebuilt.

Anti-depressants ruin one's whole life. Not feeling, not knowing what to think and living a lie.

HAZE OF THE LATTER DAYS

God made us male and female. It is important for women to be feminine and men to be masculine.

In those years I persevered but then later, a new house and state living around patriots/good cheer.

Anti-Trumps are so dumb especially after he killed ISIS and boost the economy making it plum: Shut-up bums!

Elizabeth Warren says liberals are the heart of the democratic party. If that is the case it's really dirty.

The left has free rein to destroy whatever it doesn't like and the police will do nothing about it.

We're not racist cuz we support Trump and so what if white America got him in?

It's ok for a man to dress nice/wear makeup but not for a woman? How twisted, hard to imagine.

The anti-racism Antifa are the violent ones but that is wrongthink for these liberal left hoodlums.

I love dressing up and wearing makeup but feminists tell me that's a sellout.

Since there's nothing worse than a woman's scorn the masculine female can be terrifying/forlorned.

These guys are glib, they talk a good game but it's textbook Alinsky and they're shysters in the main.

Amazing to see her sermons in the eighties compared to how she is now after taking a public fall.

HAZE OF THE LATTER DAYS

They're afraid to be feminine--stylish, tender, clean--but are expected to get tattoos and be mean.

For masculine power women stayed fat. They misconstrued power to mean size but it's the opposite.

Masculine: getting the job done. Feminine: propping them up hon.

It is normal to be fascinated by the opposite sex, it's the birds and the bees not this current hex.

Their echo chamber peer group will push em over the edge, always negotiating false meanings.

Wearing makeup is fun, even high heals if that's what you want. Don't listen to em, they're the sellouts.

The antifa actually think we're the fascists and they're guilt free. They're against slavery you see.

They are so violent and crude but can't see it. We're the fascists but they're nice, into freedom.

The church is endowed by God but managed by men which means doubt and confusion.

Tho' it appears they're winning we just have to proceed as if they're not, and they're not--it's all spinning.

The division is Christ vs. self or in-group focus.

Thank God we're not slaves of peer pressure. We have an inner compass and rely on the Comforter.

Social hypnotic is a raging river sucking you into it. Must be strong to stand for Trump/not submit.

HAZE OF THE LATTER DAYS

Why a fence and a locked gate? Cuz then you're happy every day and no one destroys your fate.

If conservative you're an individual and not part of the club, but we loners will always love Trump.

Very clever and so much like Hitler: The Nazi fascists say it's US but we resist, being mentally fitter.

They virtue signal how nice they are and they want acceptance: this explains the liberal menace.

They have no wisdom or knowledge of how things work so they just seek to be with the clique of jerks.

Having collapsed lines between good and evil they fail to distinguish the righteous from bad people.

Fake media is the megaphone of the Trump-loathing left.

Don't overburden the flock with ceremony and spiritual anxiety coming from meetingitis and social status.

Many meetings: I just wanna love God not deal with snide it's a brick to carry not a lamp to guide.

Someone finds God and innocently joins a church. He now has a brick to carry not a lamp to guide, yuk!

How I see you is not a reflection of myself. The perceiver and the perceived are not the same, pal.

If I see you as bad it doesn't mean I am bad. We are separate, not one as you've been told or read.

Birds of a feather become an echo chamber then you're sure you're right while in great error.

Man is an adaptive animal, so the sweeter his wife the more he'll succeed, thrive and be phenomenal.

A bunch of dumb idiots complementing each other--taking pictures like the red carpet, suckers.

Tell someone they're a victim enough times and they soon want revenge.

Hollywood: "'we're bored with the concept of right and wrong."

Arminians would hate the inerrancy of scripture since that's God overruling the free will of man.

Once inerrancy is questioned a whole host of errors follow.

Once Arminianism takes root the cancer of humanism creeps into the church.

How Calvinism built American government: Not trusting fallen man/restraining em.

Arminianism leads to statism: man-made government independent of God in pursuit of "paradise".

Representative checks-and-balance system is from Calvinism: not trusting em.

Calvinism is the most influential constitutional strain in all U.S. history.

"Justice" is a youth cause. In a rational world, it's freedom of speech, expression, individual rights/laws.

HAZE OF THE LATTER DAYS

Don't see evil as having the upper hand just cuz they're loud. God's on our side and sin He disallows.

Arminian heresy is that God loves everybody. That's a lie, He hated many cuz they were so shady.

U.S. rule of law, prosperity with freedom: very unique in world history.

Humanistic Statism: a reliance on other men and institutions rather than God.

The Messianic State: The belief that the state will rescue them.

Arminianism is so individualistic it leads to a mass egalitarian "democratic" system which is chaos.

Every man for himself, chaos, egalitarianism = someone climbs to the top: tyranny.

Free will makes man superior over a sovereign God on the issue of salvation. Free will is modern insanity.

You know you're winning the information war when the other side has no response but censorship.

The startling differences between liberal and conservative explains it all, why relationships failed.

They'll stop at nothing to destroy our western civilization—our monuments, our statues, Mt. Rushmore.

The left is internationalist and they control the narrative so it's down with statues/we're sick over it.

HAZE OF THE LATTER DAYS

These people are so violent and they want revenge. Is that your kids, your spouse, your aunts?

They don't protest cliteroectomies but statues--always the wrong view.

Nothing to say, parroting points, garbage.

Confidence is very appealing. Try to please everyone and you'll please no one or hurt feelings.

With each populist head chopped, into the swamp he is sucked.

Supposed to be equal protection under the law, not only favored viewpoints.

It's viewpoint discrimination.

GLOBALISM AND ISLAM

Another psychotic inbred royal calling himself a communist is threatening America: North Korea

50 physicians/researchers writing about cancer cells in vaccines found dead in last five years, it said.

CHINA: "You move against N. Korea and we'll attack you." That's the biggest story of all too.

They see California and say "all of that is what the whites stole from us and we'll make it better"--HAH.

Jerry Brown says he's an environmentalist but says we should be like China who is the dirtiest?

It's fallible, twisted, arrogant, globalist, corporate power chiefs in control of demagogues and thieves.

HAZE OF THE LATTER DAYS

While we were partying like no tomorrow, they were digging bunkers to ensure their own survival.

The greatest dangers of the A.I. are those who control it and corner the stock market around it.

We guard info not cuz we have something to hide but to protect against people like you, the snide.

Robots used for military? Of course the globalists would love it, they're the ones who control it.

Just the A.I. computers going haywire, glitching out, going outa control--it's horrifying and unimaginable.

Robots running down street killing people. I think you should be concerned about that. Elon Musk

You must be pro-active in A.I. regulation not reactive--because then it's too late. Elon Musk.

Being psychologically so poisoned you don't know still: you're losing your humanity and mentally ill.

Selfish psychotic narcissists in control of A.I. machines

Communism killed 100 million people in the last century alone.

What we're all up against: total evil wanting to break our free will, end our families and enslave us.

The bought-and-paid-for (fake globalist) news media have even blamed Trump for Barcelona.

Formula: Create a permanent underclass, radicalize them, bring down the whole, communism.

HAZE OF THE LATTER DAYS

The left, although empty, has taken on the spirit of Islam which at least has something in it.

The ideas of the ruling class are in every epoch the ruling ideas. Karl Marx

Progressives (communists, SJWs) will kick you outa your mansion and give you a box to live in.

The new left was an anti-American party from the beginning.

Goal of the twisted anti-America media: indoctrinate with ginned-up hatred, intolerance and violence.

Thought life is very narrow/shallow outside of pleasure/ego.

Goal: Stir up civil war from which Marxism, communism and totalitarianism can sweep into power.

They want us poor, divided and fighting each other so they can take over.

Antifa liberals aligned with Islam to cause bedlam so they can impose Marxism but it's globalism.

Their admitted plan: bringing incompatible groups into free societies to kill the spirit of renaissance.

Communists never refer to themselves as communists but "progressives".

Red-green alliance (communism aligned with Islam) wants to "rub the right's nose in diversity".

It's forced integration and Islamification of the West where we must convert or submit to it.

HAZE OF THE LATTER DAYS

Pansies. You're in a safe space: America. Learn to appreciate it or get out. Ben Shapiro

You call yourself micro-aggressed and now we're all supposed to fall down and beg you for forgiveness.

The globalists have abnormal goals for humanity but Putin/Trump are normals, their natural enemies.

Globalization is: colonization by devil-worshipping pedophile rings.

If you attack bigotry with violence it's not violence?

They're always in search of being offended to increase their virtue level which is never ended.

"I'm offended" is now the trump card. Ignore facts no matter how hard.

Between logic and character-assault the latter always wins, cuz once labeled a racist it's a demon.

With each populist head chopped, into the swamp Trump is sucked.

Living in America is the best any human being in world history has ever had it, yet they wanna break it.

GLOBAL PLAN: Establish angry divisions along racial lines then blame capitalism for racist crimes.

To call you a racist without evidence is a terrible thing so that should be your comeback to quislings.

Coming with a trail of trash to bash the planet and it's mankind's Nemesis-- that's the gist of it.

HAZE OF THE LATTER DAYS

My job is not to be inoffensive but tell the truth.

One punishment is suddenly being surrounded by strangers while losing our history and culture.

Caitlyn Jenner is a wealthy man with a mental disorder. Ben Shapiro

30,000 scientists agree climate change is a hoax and Al Gore made big bucks.

Your subjective self-knowledge is irrelevant to me (what you think you are) I only care what you are.

Unearned moral superiority of the middle east: they won't take em but insist we take their refugees.

The mainstream media is a disaster area, corrupt from top to bottom in America.

SJWs say being inoffensive is more important than free speech.

They say lowcarb is for GERD but animal foods cause worst acid ever.

Minimum wage will rise naturally when you stop dumping low wage workers on it to make money.

It's not fear-mongering it's the truth--you just don't wanna hear true news.

Once they vote that way, ain't my people.

The most popular topic is: immigration.

Immigration policy pre-1970: We want immigrants much better than us.

Our media is shockingly corrupt and lying to you. Ann Coulter

Alt left goals: civil war in America to overthrow Trump.

HAZE OF THE LATTER DAYS

Social justice warrior: new word for communism and they hate America and anyone who loves her.

Every American deserves a government that puts their needs first. Potus

It's the globalists behind the protests, they don't want out success cuz then their plans are bust.

They'd rather get ratings and clicks then tell the truth. Donald Trump

Watch Fox and Friends cuz that's what Potus watches

Trump is liberating our small towns from creeps like MS13, Daddy's back and it's SOOO freeing.

Who the heck are they to criticize Trump? Creeps, thugs, low-lifes, crud.

Freedom will prevail, our values will endure, our citizens will prosper and our nation will thrive like never before. Donald Trump

A war hero with cancer can still be a traitor.

We don't see skin color. Trumpster

Donald Trump stared at me, making faces. Hillary Clinton

As a result of the echo chamber more false confidence is engendered and they regroup, tortured.

Donald Trump is so incredibly riveting, I can't turn away. Alex Jones

The fake news is a wall of fraud. Everything they accuse him of, they are doing. Alex Jones

Liberal aligned with Jihadis cuz they hate the west

HAZE OF THE LATTER DAYS

When the dumb and blind will suddenly see it will be a wonderful revolution for you and me.

If her skin crawled debating Trump she was weak and a creep.

Look at what's happened to Europe. They want it to happen here!

Growing bigotry and racism among blacks in America.

Democrats are an evil party conflating the needy with the seedy.

They want the homeless tempest-tossed cuz they are making billions, at our cost.

My head says we're in terrible times but my heart says we're waking up: we're gonna fight and win.

When you know God is coming they become irrelevant as the world becomes strangely dim.

No matter what we see, God is coming and that's how we live our life.

Atrazine in the water changes the sex of amphibians.

EPILOGUE

Left's in a frenzy cuz all things they've tried have failed. It's about immaturity so it's all bungled.

They have their own youth culture but it's an echo chamber as they block out elders and stay in error.

They're trendy, chic, in the know, fresh and employed--and dead wrong/not ok.

They're followed and have a million friends. Smilers love the trends but mislead you nevertheless.

HAZE OF THE LATTER DAYS

No one cheers a white who gets off. We've lost in-group preference, the whites are trashed/lost.

Why do they hate Trump? Cuz they're left wing ideologues who wanna destroy this presidency or bust.

To escape anti-Trump fake news, people are surging into Life movies.

What is it about Trump that is read as white supremacist? Cuz he made money, what is the gist?

They call him a white supremacist no matter how many times he disavows it.

Enigma of the century: why they hate Trump.

They're not solving our problems they're just trying to push a duly elected president out of office.

In this era whites are down not up. To have a white president so successful looks racist, must stop.

They have Trump Derangement Syndrome (TDS) so will try everything and anything to bring POTUS down.

The immature babies can't take the reality switch from political correctness to common sense.

She was so humiliated by the loss she's gonna continue to throw stuff until something sticks.

Just being white is white supremacist now.

They're told to bully us, fire us, disinvite us, remove or censure us but we'll use that energy back, thanks.

HAZE OF THE LATTER DAYS

It is alienating to have the news spew out such lies about the great man answering our cries.

You can't do that because America is racist, and capitalism is racist.

"We're gonna get you, cuz it's time for us to have power, it's our revolution we didn't get with Hillary."

They know you're not racist, they implant chips on our shoulders to take control/start a race war.

America has withstood tyrants and bullies before.

Our predicament: equality, inclusiveness and diversity is now superseding the first amendment.

They've created the rage mob and now they can't control the rage mob (children living with mom).

Democrats keep everyone focused on identity politics so we don't see their scams and tricks.

Debate feeds demons and drains believers.

Say what you need to say and cut if off. Don't debate it's too draining for the day.

Conserve your energy/don't let em rob it. It's your reality/God's behind it.

Everyone wants to argue with you--one sign you're right so enjoy your day with just a few.

Though you were swept up through social hypnotism to accept this filthy stuff, you will still be judged.

They can't have it, Trump won. They can't handle that so burn it all down.

HAZE OF THE LATTER DAYS

If we beat this civil war and unite, 50 years of prosperity. Lose it, hell on earth and not maybe.

What will enemies do when we're tied down in a civil war?

They mistake our restraint for weakness but let dog off the chain, we flatten em with fighting genius.

They switched from Russia to race and they're going full force with that--so gear up, dig in, brace.

They know they're done so redouble efforts foaming at the mouth bar none.

George Washington freed his slaves and made financial arrangements yet Antifa is in a rage.

Abolish memory if it's all bad for you. These are satan's anchors to evil that Jesus erased too.

It wasn't you it was a demon but you were weak enough to let him in.

Died in fact then came back with a Creative Act.

The more energetic and spiritual the more horrible if you're a conduit to evil for then it's real.

It should be a great relief to know it was a demon not you acting horrible, ruthless or unfeminine.

The dross is stripped away by hard work and media attention.

Cuza the things I was doing I kept company with demons until a prayer to Jesus gave me freedom.

Cuz it's my job, a short quip resolves contradiction and it's like every one is an accomplishment.

HAZE OF THE LATTER DAYS

How'd you get the demon? It's from who you hang with and what they think--bad associations stink.

If they believe this crap they buy the whole map and they're gonna bring you down that's a fact.

If you're gonna go back ten years, why not 20 or 30? Don't get stuck cuz evil anchors are bad luck.

Global warming--are you kidding? They are globalist pawns and may believe in perversity/sinning.

The trendies are frenemies and that's how they've been through the centuries.

You've reached a point where you can't let anyone in. Formal invitations, locked gate, create from within.

I hated the government schools. I felt surrounded by fools and they were bullies too, lewd and cruel!

These people would invade without calling, sleep on the floor, invite all their friends and start wars.

The most important change in my life was a locked gate. You cant get to me again/change my fate.

Globalist pawns are boring cum-bay-yah zombie creations and they don't make good friends.

Liberals restrict your freedom and privacy and are very controlling: On the take, deceiving.

I'm a hyper-evolute. I faced the challenge and overcame by purifying and dividing from the loose/lewd.

You threw me to the wolves but I overcame and survived, I'm the best and have hyper-evolved.

HAZE OF THE LATTER DAYS

Feel the victory and the mystery, it is His story.

If they believe the new age things they buy the whole list. Don't waste time, climb, seek God's kiss.

Where are the Christian men of valor, warriors for God? All worn down, part of the world, odd.

Have no peers if they're gonna act like that.

Catholicism is now universalism--anyone can be saved, all paths ok even Chrislam.

Falling away has made church unrecognizable.

By default, if you're not serving the most high you're serving the most low.

Seek your core essential, the quintessential: more pure of all.

There's no fear in dissing Christians and what we believe, but in dissing Islam it's the end without reprieve.

Marriage gave me needed protection so that I could live again and create without fearing interruption.

Don't pray for money and power but that the book changes culture for the better.

If everyone's on the red carpet then no one's on the red carpet can't you see that?

Relaxation is like putting money into a bank or insurance. It's food and sustenance priming success.

When the Creative Act is complete it's like ocean going through the veins: now return to the beginn

HAZE OF THE LATTER DAYS

POLITICS

He's not only bad cuz he's a liar, but cuz he doesn't inspire. Rosie O'Donnell on Donald Trump

I'll scratch you off my list, what an idiot. Thus proving: no lower intellect can ever judge a higher intellect.

Get used to being ignored until that moment you POP into the scene, world.

Don't devolve to attention-getting to compensate for your as-yet-unrecognized genius tho' I know it's frustrating.

It will never end cuz if you don't manage negative stimuli (snowflake yourself) you become more panicked.

Less and less is required to trigger you more and more and you end up controlling everyone/abhorrent.

Pedophilia and racism do not exist. It's only good vs. evil that causes hell-- what the low people pick.

Poisons get in through food and clothes so avoid those but firstly stick to what you know in our Bible.

We took the blame for the whole thing completely forgetting all the slimy things they were doing.

He was a great foil for me. Stark opposites, all his different qualities showed mine by contrast, see?

If one rejects you for your words, then they determine your reality, actions, limits, everything--walk away.

Rejects you for saying something (crossing her lines) but then she comes back, forget her this time.

Say something wrong, lose friend. They come back like nothing happened but censorship/86ed: drop em.

FRENEMY

Nagging problem: Flaky associates bring constant disappointments so reject this disrespect.

We're nice until we're not then watch out, nuts.

Lotsa saved people caught up with the devil: broken lives, broken homes, evil.

The problem with masochists is when they meet a real sadist.

Be sin free and life becomes perfect too. Don't expect disaster/failure as in the past (just learning tools).

Don't keep remorsing back to lower levels when you didn't know better and filled with demons/fetters.

Possibly a demon for years because of which you acted out, became maudlin or a lush and a louse.

With experience/time you find what works best (FOR YOU) then expand those while deleting the others.

The new cumbaya church music is shallow, emotional, fleshly, sounds the same and is man-centered.

"Quality worship"--from tingle to tingle, search for greater tingle--praise and worship with co-mingle.

All you can do is repent then do what you do best and forget the rest.

Though past doesn't exist it can still make you sick. Forgive yourself for when used by demons, hick.

Things aren't obvious until they are, so be patient and suddenly they'll see afar.

Jesse P. said to treat all thoughts as evil, of the devil--don't trust em but be like cats/dogs, living now.

Ain't no big thing to wait for the bell to ring. Until that ring, nothing. Grace Jones

HAZE OF THE LATTER DAYS

Style/strength can't be faked. You either have it or you don't yet not thru birth but correcting mistakes.

HIPPY

Go to college with the SJW mob: Come out traumatized with no job.

College traumatized me suddenly. Professors were debauched, hated America, made me think their way.

Trump Derangement Syndrome PART 2: Conservatives feel crazy cuz they lost family over voting this way.

America's coming into it's harvest under Donald Trump, God's anointed. It's payback time: know it.

Obama accused Trump of old political theories as if he were superior destroying America forever.

Great biographies are fascinating--most died in tragedy after magnificent opulence and notoriety.

We're moving legally from "intent" matters to only "consequences" matter-- legal system is in tatters.

Microaggression: any act that makes the listener uncomfortable regardless of the intent?

Don't trust thoughts, they're of the devil and the past is gone/doesn't exist. Be just here now like dogs/cats.

Only one cure for SJWs and college profs: put em in an Iranian prison to learn about tyranny vs. freedom

Not all ideologies are expressions of psychiatric disorder but many are.

FIRST THEY IGNORE YOU

First they ignore you then they laugh at you then they fight you then you win. Gandhi.

HAZE OF THE LATTER DAYS

They've so conditioned people to conform that a thinker is totally out of sync and it makes us sick.

When the wicked rule the people mourn. Trump's made us cool though they're tearing him down.

They're making their move--that's why all this evil stuff is happening--so be patient while Trump removes.

CNN advocates for "free press" then protests we be censored.

Heh, God set em up for the kill by tracking em into the virtual world. Maybe we will win, ya know?

How to stop abuse: You take control of the time he spends with--so he can't disappoint, the louse.

Trumps SMV (Sexual Market Value) is just too high as charming/smart billionaire. They can't stand it/gaps too wide.

Trump tells the bloody truth/unthinkingly while Obama gave em a ruse as a big phony/smilingly.

The press isn't the enemy of the people but the fake news (80%) is. Donald Trump

If we show black-on-white crime the media bans us and it's the same in Europe when Islam stabs us.

These people are evil and they're making their move. Alex Jones

Liberals: 6 x more likely to steal, 9 x less likely to give but 1000 x more like to *say* they're giving.

WHAT IS LIBERTY?

When people get weak the first thing they seek is power and there is the devil promising forever.

Major mechanism in the renewal of conservatism is: resurgence of the nation state.

HAZE OF THE LATTER DAYS

What is liberty? The right to tell people what they don't want to hear and remain totally free.

No logic to a demon other than destruction and your ruination so stop remorsing back and just forget him.

Wash this generation off. It's a gritty smelly dark aura of ugly mauve tones and living with it is very rough.

Can't stand hearing the lies anymore. It's too frustrating and why should I be debased by the whore?

California isn't my country anymore and it won't be until I'm dead--and it makes me sad. John Steinbeck

No black in power has ever been able to help the black community but a white man did who they hated.

Whoever has guns has the power. When it's just government it's not a true democracy and a dire hour.

FEMINISTS HATE DADDY TRUMP

Trump has been chosen by God to weed corruption. Open borders means one thing: hostile INVASION.

I will clean up the darkness and usher in the light, for I have America in My Hand. The Lord

For Christians praying for impeachment/death of our wonderful God-given president: hell swallows em.

The smart say democrats will never see the Whitehouse again. This red tsunami is due to their deep sin.

I'm so thrilled at the morality of our president: 15,000 pedophiles arrested yet the news never reports it.

This is the year of major arrests including Hillary/Obama so get ready for catastrophe/social unrest.

About to have the biggest energy explosion in our history. Big companies are moving back, gladly.

Why do they call him a racist when he's the most non-racist president we've ever had? Makes us mad.

Arrogant liberals always talking about their "rights" but what about their wrongs? Disgusting.

97% of news posts on Donald Trump are negative. Due to constitution, we must put up with it.

It's gonna be a red tsunami nationwide so get ready for major arrests of traitors, crooks and pedophiles.

America's set up right now to be the number one producer of ENERGY in 2019.

Initially Trump was to resume his empire after 4 but after seeing the deep corruption it'll be 8 years.

We're outraged after John McCain's glittering funeral turned into a Trump bashing session.

COMMIE

White people were so sweet with their little pets, roses and other plants. Revive our race, save us yet.

But we're nice to the point of maudlin masochism as we gladly give what is theirs to rapacious invaders.

In the human species it is insanity to care more about out-group than in-group members.

Pros and cons of multiculturalism: One the one hand more beheadings, on the other interesting cuisine.

Multiculturalism: The first bits are interesting then the returns slow down then the problems, profound.

HAZE OF THE LATTER DAYS

The traveling couple who said evil didn't exist were then killed by ISIS terrorists.

Wherever masses of humans = massive fecal matter but open border liberals don't care about splatter.

Be aware of social impact of stepping over homeless and their feces while exploring the city. Paris Trip Advisory

Poor Germans and their recent guilt complexes apologizing for everything they say and think/stop this.

Confusion is two parallel news universes and that's why it's like we speak two separate languages.

Socialism is philosophy of failure, creed of ignorance, gospel of envy, whose virtue is equal sharing of misery. Winston Churchill

Paris looks more like a bazaar for illegal migrants. Paris trip advisor review

They care more about the extinction of the mold beetle than white people.

Economic migrants become a client group the state controls. Despite murder and rape it's power ya know.

Leaked Soros docs confirm migrant crisis a tool of "global governance". Good grief wake up, liberal dunces.

Swedish rape stats show 80% are foreign born.

The elites push migrant policies where they're not bearing the brunt of the resulting catastrophes.

COLLECTIVE PUNISHMENT ISN'T JUSTICE

The current mode is collective punishment which is the opposite to justice.

Macron agrees Europe needs 600 MILLION migrants in the next 30 years, he's the Kalergi Plan enforcer.

HAZE OF THE LATTER DAYS

We don't want em here cuz we know **MAL-ADAPTATION** to insane or loose environments is the end of us.

Tip for hot Paris trip: don't step in the shit.

To repeat. Macron: In the next 30 years 600 **MILLION MORE** are coming but we have Trump who we adore.

Once western culture becomes the minority view you won't have free speech or women's rights ever again.

How do race hustlers get power and wealth? By yelling "racist" that's how.

To find out who rules over you find out who you're not allowed to criticize.

With time the only thing worth talking about can't be talked about.

Signs of radically changed demography: Bags of shit on Frisco sidewalks, bags of body parts in NYC, yuk.

Whites, please have babies. We don't like--we abhor--these cruel brutal cultures with different realities.

They want us all brown, period. One big bag of it easily malleable and accepting of tyranny/used to it.

These people lack empathy and have totally different values when it comes to dear animals/go to hell!

When it comes to animals even the tender mercies of the wicked are cruel.

They love and enjoy working in meat packing industries. Have you ever wondered why, softies?

While flooded with disparate cultures making us sick all we can do is fence up and live our own trip.

THEY HATE ANYTHING OLD

They change the four olds: Old ideas, old culture, old customs and old habits but we don't want this.

HAZE OF THE LATTER DAYS

We console ourselves in this terrible period by pretending it's not going on.

Thomas Jefferson's version of fake news: the "lies of the day"

Because of Trump, veterans are the new elites. Feminists with comfy existence should just shut up, the creeps.

Photos make us vulnerable since they're so into looks/critical and we're more into the spiritual (invisible).

It's phony, scary, weird, fake happy, so boring everyone's smiling, say nothing misery camaraderie.

What are they laughing about? It's a phony social glue or veneer smoothing reality with other fakers.

It's always grit on my nerves, hysterical laughing like the cackling of thorns hiding such darkness, forlorned.

Liberalism is a mental illness and if you have to adapt to it (like boss or spouse) you become crazy.

The fake virtue signaling left are always moralizing yet stand for the lowest evils and debaucheries. *How I overcame: Daily Fasting not Counting*

The possibilities are endless if you think like this. Just wait, you'll be discovered in fastarian bliss.

TYRANTS AND PROCRASTINATORS

Tho' enthused at first the flame dies and he goes slow, gets lazy, doesn't know, has no empathy for y'all.

Enthused at first then they flake out. Happy to promise/plan then becomes cold, zombie, a different man.

No staying power, weak foundation, limp handshake, vacillates--that's the immature man/THIRD RATE.

He always thinks he can do it, explosive acceptance--but then distracted by whatever catches his glance.

HAZE OF THE LATTER DAYS

If they know how important it is to you that's precisely when they'll withdraw/withhold giving it.

Progressives caught in a "purity spiral" of demanding more and more strict adherence to their bull.

LASCIVIOUS LIBERALISM

There is relentless dishonesty in the very people paid highly to inform us.

Why think you're helping the kids who are grandstanding and you're going along with their manipulation?

How are university professors helping, allowing attention-getting narcissistic undergrads taking over class?

"Emancipatory Politics" is hexed as it "repairs" discriminated groups and puts down dominant whites.

Everyone does it, it's always been that way, you have your sins too. That's the three con jobs for you.

Liberals are calling names while conservatives make arguments--no connection so be done with em.

The worst thing you can do is tell mentally ill liberals that they're brilliant, entitled and deceived.

You think they're all nice? This isn't the fifties--these are the latter days and it's scary as God repays.

Soaps: They wanna lure us in with a love story of conflict, then slip in pure debauchery and the deviant.

THEY DEGENERATE TOGETHER

People are sick and getting sicker as they all degenerate together. Seen thru the eyes of God it's a horror.

God is purity, order, goodness. Not this mess coming over the human race creating such nastiness.

HAZE OF THE LATTER DAYS

TV has a moral responsibility because people copy everything they see unless firmly grounded in morality.

The world cannot hate you but it hates Me because I testify of it that its works are evil. John 6: 7:7

Don't argue with people on the other side. Save yourself a lot of energy: avoid leftists and the snide.

I'm not speaking again, they're too mean. They have no knowledge, they wanna get back, they are fiends.

When will everyone get past the peer pressure and admit it is true?

I see y'all falling away into occult, false teachings and debauchery. This shows weakness/lack of mastery.

Totally dangerous: We want to be liked more than telling the truth.

The young liberals don't do great things for recognition but tend to fall into victimhood for validation.

Obloquy: Widespread censure or abuse; disgrace resulting from this.
In this generation, anonymity is safety.

Nazis were socialists, the KKK were democrats and the white man freed the slaves.

Secret societies like Masons lowers Christ in the scheme of things or puts Him equal with other gods.

"Those who stand for nothing will fall for anything". That is so true and I saw that in many friends I knew.

NORMALIZING PERVERSION

Or if they say "it's always been that way", normalizing perversion--hit the road/avoid destruction.

Everyone does it, it's always been that way, you have your sins too: Normalizing sin by liberal friends of you.

HAZE OF THE LATTER DAYS

They've been so cut off from their destiny they're little barbarians, shallow roots adapting to ruffians.

If you don't go along with them they censure you, de-platform you and then go after your banking.

There is no end to perversion until Jesus puts an end to it. it's depthless, fathomless, bottomless.

You're riding a wave cuz that's the current narrative but wait till things change--you'll face what you did.

Let God take care of things, it'll be much worse for your enemies. Vengeance is His, the best--believe me.

Comedians can't tell unapproved jokes, scientists must abandon politically unpopular research.

Wherever democracy is allowed the progressive globalist left is doomed. They know that, terrified too.

THE DEAD VOTE DEMOCRAT

The dead vote democrat.

I too was entrenched in the dirty generation and came back to reality taking the values of grandma and God.

American-hating forces have come out of the woodwork to stop the recovery--wanting us down, not up.

Stop telling our wonderful president to "tone it down". He'll lose his great personality: why he won.

Don't you dare tone it down President Trump! We love your sass/you have class, please keep it up!

The left says: "I want to feel good about myself so I'll MAKE them do something generous on my behalf."

Dear Mr. Trump: Please do not tone down your speech, be more harsh, please.

HAZE OF THE LATTER DAYS

THE IRONY OF THE LEFT

The irony of the left: They tell us what we're seeing with our own eyes doesn't exist so why are we pist?

Nazis killed 150+ million people and they call us Nazis? What an insult, don't let em do this, it's crazy.

Trump: Beautiful deals with democrats or warlike retaliation for probes? You choose: he loves or scolds.

Truth mixed with error is still error. The problem is mixture.

Antifa's home invasion will make Tucker more popular than ever as the Streisand effect takes over.

CONSERVATIVE MEDIA SLIDES LEFT

I will never watch FOX again except for Tucker, Hannity and Ingraham--the others have sold out, friends.

Trump has done more this country than ever in history and you ingrates hate him still, hot coals of treachery.

Trump and cronies have it all in a bag. Thousands are going to prison and we'll recall you arrogant cads.

If you're into occult--a Christian believing in reincarnation, a nut--you should be afraid of hell and repent.

When things finally turn around and the criminals are in jail we'll recall how you flaked out and failed.

After 8 years of the trauma of Obama, that's it--we're at our end! Pray for clarity and perseverance friends.

When Facebook isn't banning you they're blocking your likes! You don't know who loves you/who hates.

You don't have to explain cuz if you explain you put yourself on their level, way down with the devil.

HAZE OF THE LATTER DAYS

The center left is collapsing as it's cut to half or less. People want tradition back cuz this means happiness.

PROGRESSIVE IS ANTI-TRADITION

Progressive underground is anti-tradition and based on the 60's sexual liberation movement.

It's the total destruction of the Old Order based on Christianity and the moral absolutes implied.

It's the ushering in of an occult new age. A socialistic kingdom of conformity to an illusion of falsehoods.

It's a Pantheistic New World Order on earth and it's fancy illusions combined with fascistic communism.

FOX: Anti-Trump stuff ticked me off but now it's ramped up: Tucker and Hannity face a hostile environment.

Apparently blacks will love you if you're a lying corrupt person giving them free stuff as evil is called "good".

Reason for mass riots of young men across the world: it's our fault for not giving opportunities/more?

My best advice was: let Trump do his job. For unobstructed that's his genius, didn't you know?

At least Mussolini made the trains run on time but De Blasio makes nothing run on time. Michael Savage

Yes I do have fun exposing these people, to reveal how vacuous and moronic they really are.

Thank God for our president, it's our blessed destiny to experience it before going over the edge.

HOSTILE INVASION OF YOUNG MEN

DROP EM if they say "everyone does it" or "you have your sins too".

HAZE OF THE LATTER DAYS

Low IQ cultures: trash, violence. High IQ cultures: clean order and refinement.

21st Century warfare is using millions of people as political weapons.

Import the third world, become the third world--simple as that.

Everything we are--our very selves--will be lost if we turn the country over to people who are not us!

Nationalism: Pride in neat clean streets, happiness. Globalism: Trash everywhere/mean creeps.

Yes diversity is nice--music and food--but that's as long as they stay unique, not globalist pawns/freaks.

What is a traitor? One who prefers outsiders!

Nationalism is the opposite to patriotism? Why are they listed as synonyms, Mr. Macron?

DIVERSITY MEANS: LESS WHITE PEOPLE

Diversity means: less white people.

Low IQ pops: Trashy and violent. High IQ pops: Pristine cities and villages, respectful and decent.

Macron took a WWI memorial event as his chance to take a swipe at Trump's vision (anti-global) nationalism.

WWI Memorial to the millions of men who died for nationalism against which Macron grandstands?

Americans will never knowingly adopt socialism but through liberalism will accept it all. Norman Thomas

We fight to defend our home/bill of rights--anything else is a racket and organized crime. Smedley Butler

HAZE OF THE LATTER DAYS

Armies, debts/taxes are the instruments bringing the many under the domination of the few. James Madison

When the whole world lives in your country nothing survives. Mixing means ALL traditions worn away.

The native people of a land should never be made a minority within it. Shoot me, I must be a bigot.

Higher IQs make them harder to deceive, keep in captivity or control. That's the west when we were bold.

THE HARDY ARE HARD TO OPPRESS

Citizens of the west are historically the hardest to rule over or oppress--we have the right to self-defense.

SHARIA is brutality we hate (and gives us nightmares at night) because we believe in human rights.

We don't care about tweets we just want the wall, that's all.

Affluent liberals in power never think about this travesty. They're in white gated communities neat/orderly.

The higher the IQ the more gentle/genteel, the lower the more rapacious, animalistic and unempathic.

This isn't about replacing us, oh no. This is about helping people who are less fortunate/living low.

You went through that cuz you hadn't learned boundaries. Without that the world flows in, evil cronies.

Attitude of mine: I don't wear a gun cuz I hate the people outside but because I love the people inside.

Tell the nutty: Baptized globalism (open borders and amnesty) is worlds apart from biblical Christianity.

HAZE OF THE LATTER DAYS

Southern Border: It's always a serious thing when the military's called in: very good or very bad.

If music and drama is to satisfy everyone it won't satisfy anyone.

Merkel and Mae care only for outsiders, not insiders--and that is mental illness in the human herd, traitors.

PAY EM TO LEAVE

UK: Paying em all to leave would be a helluva lot cheaper than allowing em to stay so save England, ok?

Pay em to get rid of em--the only answer for Londonstan and the rest of em--or we're dead, the white man.

Tolerance, openness and diversity now sends England back to the 7th century.

You know it all anyway, we're going to hell. That's surrounded by strangers who don't share our values.

Soros wants Israel removed saying it doesn't have a right to exist and if you criticize this you're anti-semitic?

Border Hassle: If you throw rocks it'll be treated as if it was a rifle! Pres. Trump

Elites are collapsing the third world so they can take over with tyranny. Everyone poor, the top bossy.

Curious funding streams.

There are people who want to take countries we love to hell in a handcart with no breaks. Katie Hopkins

It doesn't matter if we're poor, in shambles, invaded in our own homes because we're "culturally enriched".

Eastern Europeans have maintained the "tragic sense of life" and won't let them in but we've forgotten.

Why welcome people who don't share our values? Can you tell me this, if it destroys me and you?

TRUE CHRISTIANITY IS ORTHODOXY

Without orthodoxy a church is open to leaven, false religion and heretical concepts of pagan women.

Open Satanism in teachings/schools and government departments is destroying our churches.

Orthodox Christianity is united against treachery while most Protestants are swept along blindly.

I won't step foot in cum-bay-yah new age churches, I think with true orthodoxy I'd be open to it.

The stupidest couple I ever met became elders in their new age church called "Christian Center".

Open Satanism in teachings/schools and government departments is destroying our churches.

Orthodox Christianity is united against treachery while most Protestants are swept along blindly.

Without orthodoxy a church is open to leaven, false religion and heretical concepts of pagan women.

I won't step foot in cum-bay-yah new age churches, I think with true orthodoxy I'd be open to it.

The stupidest couple I ever met became elders in their new age church called "Christian Center".

THE DIVERSITY RELIGION

Diversity is the religion of our time. It's like "we are one" which is a lie while destroying our very lives.

HAZE OF THE LATTER DAYS

The EU was a Nazi plan--paradise of the future. It's not Trump who is nazi it is Macron, tyrant for hire.

I'm aware of the cosmic vision and it's communism. I was taken in too, long ago while I was still fishin'

The end of May and Merkel is here, symbolizing the stupidity of emotional women causing ruin/fear.

The glories of multiculturalism is sad illusion when in fact it's ghettos of POCs who hate each other.

Rights of Muslim communities not to be offended are greater than our rights to free speech. Katie Hopkins

500 million more: Why we hate Macron (toxic weasel) even more than Merkel and May, angels of treason.

To the new age, "universal values" means debauchery, loss of freedom and privacy, invasion by nasty.

Free market capitalism has been the greatest wealth-creating engine in the history of the world.

World poverty has gone down from 70% to 10% not from socialism but from free-market capitalism.

No one EVER flees free market capitalism to go back to socialism. Would they go back to Venezuela?

POLI-PSYCH UPDATES

In these impeachment trials we need an attack dog not a cat bath [kissing their ass]. Matt Gaetz

They gotta obsess over Trump cuz they don't really have an agenda to help Americans. Matt Gaetz

They're idea of "normal" is a deranged focus on Donald Trump: always returning to normal, duds.

HAZE OF THE LATTER DAYS

If gungrabber Biden succeeds he'll leave it in the hands of people who will aggress on your home, see.

They're making Jan. 6 much worse than it is but will make it a holiday signaling attacks by insurgents.

Does it concern you I watch war documentaries not "positive" things? They're reality to me.

Impeachment: 64% think it's a joke, only 15% watch it all but MOST don't wanna watch any of it at all.

THE TRUE RACISM NOW

RACISM is truly our greatest threat and challenge: white men are being erased, debased and fired.

This president is totally for slaughtering innocent children in the womb/wants us to agree to it too.

As the stomping of free speech continues drip by drip, we can't say "Chinese Virus" or it's a guilt trip.

They're trying to make us feel bad that we ever voted for Donald Trump: delegitimized by chumps.

They want us to think they have the moral upper hand. And you know what? They don't God said.

I love Donald Trump/support all his policies but especially love his STYLE-- what they call criminal.

How many millions don't like Donald Trump cuz the others don't like Donald Trump? Mental chumps.

[China spy] Bang-Bang's boyfriend actually tried to make a case against Trump, a married man.

Saying "we will never give up, we will never give in" is now criminalized cuz our great president said it.

HAZE OF THE LATTER DAYS

Liberals and the political class hear celebrities and think: "I'll base my entire political opinion on that!"

Burn a church, they'll hang a BLM banner on the wall but burn the banner it's proof you burned it all.

HEALTH UPDATES

Frig contains: grape juice, pineapple juice, V8 juice. That's all I need and I'm never hungry.

Due to rough beginnings [father walking out on him] he loved booze and food which killed him.

If you feel sick could it be the shirt you're wearing? Always check ingredients/no synthetics.

SUGAR BOX on desk contains: gummy bears, cliff bars, dates and saltine crackers for gut aches.

How'd I know I was born a choker and would finally end up on juices? For some food's a poison, obvious.

Rather than diet control they go on drugs like proton inhibitors or sleep masks for apnea, yuk!

BIRDLIKE ENGINES EAT FRUGAL

I'm a birdlike engine existing on sugar water. Before this I was a burper and ant-acid taker but no more.

They shovel it in for dinner, all chokers: steak, pasta, bread, fats, dips/chips and fatty desserts.

Never once do they address the solution of daily fasting to control acid reflux, it's always more drugs.

Oh I might have a few Cheetos just for the taste, big deal. Best not to get crazy over this ya' know.

HAZE OF THE LATTER DAYS

All that fiber is a menace like a truck in the gut. With elders fish is digestible if eaten weekly [once].

Let's say we really do need a little animal protein. Fish once a week covers that possibility ya see.

One never knows when he will be done until he is done. Albert Einstein.

An artist never noticed while alive becomes obsessed with being remembered after her death.

They're what you call "essential truths". Aesthetic knowledge you know underneath too.

DIETARY CONFUSION WORKSHEET

To complete a huge Creative Act I had to be strong to sustain it--why I'm always looking for the right diet.

I don't wanna be a fat vegan from eating avocados, nutbutters, chocolates and coconut creams.

If Middle Eastern continents can live on bread with near-zero glycation then we can, it's so easy man.

I wanna be slim and cut and that comes from <10 fat in the diet and that's next to zero in its influence on ya.

Soon I realized I hadn't eaten all day--I was so glycogen filled I had full satiety = no hunger, ok?

Skin fat/clumps, blood fat/sludge. That's a few of the ways fat is worn on the greasy body after you indulged.

STARCH SOLUTION AND GUT PAIN

I thought bread and jam were the problem--no, they were good. It was butter making me a big lug.

You can have sugar, honey, maple syrup or dried fruit with your bread. We need glucose but not lard.

The starch solution didn't work either. Gut pain is intense from grains, another popular diet kicked to curb.

Put all the grains in the basement and get the nutbutters back up in the kitchen--no pain with them.

But the fats increase glycation which is kept low through the grains. I decided to go with: LOW PAIN.

Back to plant fats just to have something to eat. Diet science has many contradictions, replete.

Thought I'd die from the grains. After two weeks the gut pain was excruciating but fruits/fats are comfy.

Nuts don't cause gut pain being paleo but GRAINS tear it up for real, being late agricultural/industrial.

Rotate: Fix the gut thru nutbutters and avo then go back to grains for low glycation--reversals alternating.

Even oatmeal seemingly so soft and comforting causes gut pain excruciating and I'm dam well thru with em.

Now I'm thinking: I'll take the nutbutters causing glycation and compensate thru fasting or grain alternating.

I'd hate to think the only answer is to eat meat but that's all that's left my pained gut is saying, dismayed.

FOOD AND INTELLECT

Deal with glycation, acid mucus, toxic acid crystals and the like thru intermittent fasting alone you think?

Been on every single diet and gotten sick after a time with all of em. Solution: REVERSE between em.

No more bread, rice, cereals, beans or potatoes. I'm done with starch for now as my stomach groans.

HAZE OF THE LATTER DAYS

Most don't care what they eat, many can't get enough anyway, a few obsess over what it should be.

Will I end up on meat by default, being allergic to all other foods except a little fruit? I mustn't, I cannot.

The starch solution works for most but those with sensitive guts are KILLED by fiber, a menace to many.

If you can't live/be satiated with fruit/greens and starch hurts your gut, what's left? Meat or nuts.

That's why the basement's filled with nutbutters but what about glycation? They are way up there.

After a few days of FIBER my gut feels like a big silo stuffed with cement. It's very uncomfortable I lament.

I much prefer some almond butter--spoon theory--to a bunch of fiber, and my skin got dry I swear.

The only way the rice was palatable was drenched with soy sauce and then I didn't like it anyway, hah.

REVERSAL DIETING THE ONLY SOLUTION

The only way the cereal was palatable was drenched in rice milk/white sugar as advised by Durianrider.

I enjoyed the corn/peas with brown vegan gravy with mashed potatoes but even that got old ya' know.

I guess the answer is to know all the diets and the logic behind them to shift constantly between em.

I never had this problem when young and wanting to eat everything in the universe. Now it's sparse.

Dr. Gundry to Dr. MacDougal: Grains poke holes in gut then fecal matter spills out, don't you know that?

HAZE OF THE LATTER DAYS

Solution: Abandon all diet dogma and pray each day God will sustain you with daily bread or whatevah.

No anal dribbles for an old fool. Eat a lot of food once a day so thru mass evacuation it all goes through.

KELLOCKIALISMS

Much increase comes by the strength of an ox: that's 130 new psych books by Karen Kellock.

I'm done with every detail, checked/rechecked it twice. Now I'm gonna party all day/wait for God's kiss.

Stop trying to get revelation from the world or net. Seek the spiritual now—God, angels, the Great Mind.

It's a continuous spring and I don't wanna miss a thing which is why I'm always alone thinking.

Self-congratulations for all the work you have done and what you've overcome. Now starts the fun.

P.S. The reason I call em Kellockialisms is because I'm the one who came up with em.

100 KAREN KELLOCK BOOKS

AFFINITY OR MISERY
AGELESS CORNUCOPIA
AMERICA AWAKE!
AMERICA'S DAFT ERA
ARTS OF PALEO FASTING
AUTOPHAGY ON CHEATERS
BACKSTABBING NEUROTICS
BETRAYAL TRAUMA
BOOMERS AND BROKENNESS
BOOT ON NECK
CHAMPION GUIDES
COMMIE NUTHOUSE
COMMIES
COMMUNIST SPIRIT
CONTAGION OF MADNESS
CONTAGIOUS MADNESS
CULTURE CLASH BASHED
DAFT LEFT
DAILY FASTARIAN
DAM RATS
DIVERSITY IS CRUELTY
E-RACE WHITE
EVIL FREAKS (Beyond Gross)
THE END OR A BEND?
FEMALE BULLIES AND FEMI-NAZIS
FEMALE CARNALITY
FEMALE DUMB DOWN
FEMALE POWER DRIVE
FEMINISM AND RUIN 1 & 2
FIX FOR MISFITS
FOOLS & TRAMPS
FREEDOM SPEAKING
FRENEMY ENABLER
FRENEMY LIAR
FRENEMY THIEF
FRENEMY TRAITOR
TRENEMY TYRANT
GENIUS IS HELD DOWN
GLOBALISLAM
GOD USES THE FLAWED
HAZE OF THE LATTER DAYS

KAREN KELLOCK PH.D.

M.S. Political Science, San Diego State. Ph.D. in Psychology, University of California Irvine. Postdoctoral: UCI School of Medicine, Dept. of Psychiatry [NIMH Grants]. Developed the Debris Theory of Disease, a theory of system pathology in 120 books and 22 textbooks for the general public. The theory has a general formula: All disease is obstruction, all recovery is elimination, all success is attraction. The three obstructions are people, habit and food. Remove obstruction and snap to your goals, waiting in the wings.